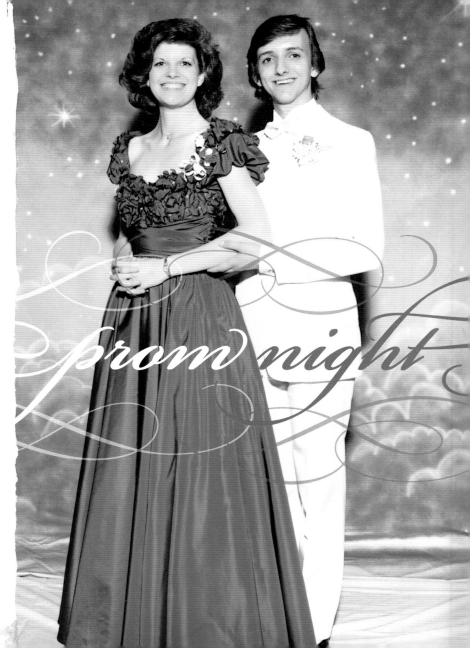

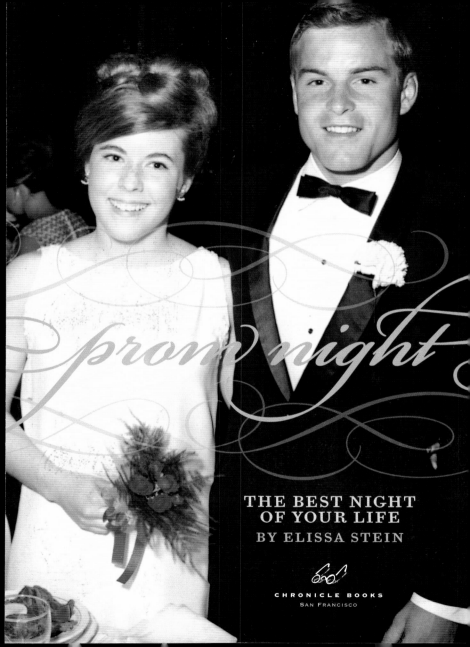

prom night

THE BEST NIGHT
OF YOUR LIFE

BY ELISSA STEIN

CHRONICLE BOOKS
SAN FRANCISCO

Library of Congress Cataloging-in-Publication Data available.
isbn: 0-8118-4544-3

Manufactured in China

Designed by Benjamin Shaykin
Typeset in Bickham Script, Bodoni Six, and Super Grotesk

Distributed in Canada by Raincoast Books
9050 Shaughnessy Street, Vancouver, British Columbia v6p 6e5

10 9 8 7 6 5 4 3 2 1

Chronicle Books llc
85 Second Street, San Francisco, California 94105
www.chroniclebooks.com

PAGE 1: Cindy Naeyaert and William Steven Saunders, Holmes County High School, Bonifay, FL, 1987. PAGE 2: Mike Meachum and Barbara Weiging, Taylor Center High School, Taylor, MI, 1968. PAGE 3: Elizabeth McDonald and David Armstrong, Oak Park High School, Oak Park, CA, 1966. OPPOSITE: Cathy and Connie Whitesell, Wissahickon High School, Ambler, PA, 1966

TO ISABEL (MY DRESS-UP QUEEN), JACKSON, AND JON

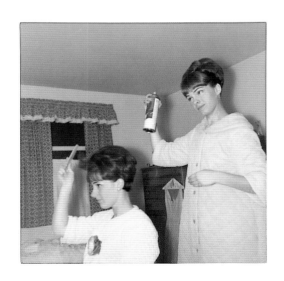

Names and date unknown

A very brief history of a very special night

1886 Short dinner jackets for formal parties first appeared at the Tuxedo Club in Tuxedo, New York. A timeless, elegant fashion statement for men was born.

1890s Proms (from promenade: a formal dance or ball) evolved as the college set graduated into the grown-up world. Eligible young men invited a society girl for prom week. The lucky young lady, chaperone in tow, would whirl from tea to dance to the grand prom finale, hoping for a marriage proposal to take home as her prize.

1910s–1930s Schools became the center of teen social life and formal dances became the place to be and be seen.

1940s–1950s Proms hit their peak. With crepe paper, balloons, and lots of imagination, students transformed their high school gyms into fantasy tableaus with popular themes along the lines of "Stardust," "Under the Sea," or "An Evening in Paris."

1960–1970s As teenagers bucked against convention, prom attendance plummeted. Wearing formal clothes while dancing to a big band just wasn't the cool thing to do. To sum it up, the movie *Carrie,* the prom story from hell, was released in 1976. However, there was one prom highlight from that era—Davy Jones taking Marcia to the prom can't be topped.

1980s Big hair and big fashion got the prom ball rolling again. Popular movies of the day, including *Footloose, Pretty in Pink,* and *Back to the Future* reflected teenagers' renewed fascination with prom night.

1990s and beyond Stretch limos, expensive attire, elaborate venues, plus the requisite pre- and post-prom activities, make for prom nights that are a far cry from the simple affairs of yesteryear.

Mary LeBeau and Larry Chiorgno
Pittsfield High School, Pittsfield, MA, 1974

Cathy Whitesell and Basil "Butch" Borzelleca
Wissahickon High School, Ambler, PA, 1966

Gregory Jackson and Julianne Wentzell
Westwood High School,
Westwood, MA, 1962

John Sheehan and Julianne Wentzell
Westwood High School,
Westwood, MA, 1963

Joanna Kerns and Daniel Rush
St. Mary of the Mount High School,
Mount Washington, PA, 1979

Elissa Stein and Rich Schneider
Massapequa High School,
Massapequa, NY, 1980

Alex Blatt and Laurel Pies
Winston Churchill High School,
Potomac, MD, 1986

Lisa Bach and Phil Hahn
Winston Churchill High School,
Potomac, MD, 1986

Ralph Schmitt and Carol Scheller
Francis Joseph Reitz High School,
Evansville, IN, 1981

Don DeCosta and Trisha Peters
College Park High School,
Pleasant Hill, CA, 1982

Michele Posner and Ben Davis
William Howard Taft High School,
Woodland Hills, CA, 1989

Annette Smith and Jerry Lamb
Urbandale High School
Des Moines, IA, 1977

TOP, L–R: **Dave Clark and Patti Dwyer,
Rosemary Tomala and Patrick Stewart,
John Kaza and Kathy Buerkle,
Jan Zelinka and Ron Stokes**
MIDDLE, L–R: **Leon Grobaski and Kathy
Foley, Dave Sonsara and Tina Gajewski,
Steve Maline and Cindy Croft,
Gary Reeve and Sharon Stockinger**
BOTTOM, L–R: **Dan Gorman and Nancy
Martens, John Schneider and Mary
Jankowski, Emory Fasano and Sharon
Fairbanks
Cherry Hill High School,
Inkster, MI, 1971**

21

Ken Anderson and Jodi Davis
Redmond High School,
Redmond, WA, 1987

RHS "A Touch of Class"
February 13, 1987
Christopher's Photography

Eddie Pasco and Kristen Davis
Redmond High School,
Redmond, WA, 1987

Regina Morrone and David Zink
Harborfields High School,
Greenlawn, NY, 1981

Carolyn Starrett and Glenn Koch
North Middlesex Regional High School,
Townsend, MA, 1982

Murray Karpen and Hilda Satkin
Passaic High School, Passaic, NJ, 1946

Karol Kane and Ron Nelson
Rich Township High School, Park Forest, IL, 1967

John Mercer, Linda Kruse, and Jeff McComb
London Central High School, Hertz, England, 1966

Roy Feinberg, Corrine Klein, Sylvia Finer, and Gerald Baron
Samuel Tilden High School, Brooklyn, NY, 1953

Curt Borders and Diane Croxton
Bushnell-Prairie City Schools, Bushnell, IL, 1977

Kathy Wilson and Jay Harris
Industrial High School, Vanderbilt, TX, 1979

Sharon Heald and Steve Phillips
Rich Township High School, Park Forest, IL, 1955

Donald Stevenson and Sheila Green
Steel High School, Steelton, PA, 1956

Rob Fish and Paula Replogle
Whitehall Yearling High School, Whitehall, OH, 1971

Andrew Kmetz and Laura Maltese
Lindenhurst High School, Lindenhurst, NY, 1967

All my love Now Karen

Lance Miklus and Dolores Russell
Roosevelt High School, Hyde Park, NY, 1967

Dixie Denham and Joseph O'Brien,
Sacred Heart High School, San Francisco, CA, 1962

Teresa Record and John Mercer
London Central High School, Hertz, England, 1966

Linda Hautala and Eric England
Thomas Jefferson High School,
Federal Way, WA, 1979

Tina Goldstein and Frank Demeri
John F. Kennedy High School,
Plainview, NY, 1981

Austin Wallace and Mary Whitfield
Northern High School, Durham, NC, 1982

Missy Vale and John Bianchi
Greenwich High School, Greenwich, CT, 1980

June 64

June 64

Amy Treadwell and Bob Wyman
Foxborough High School,
Foxborough, MA, 1977

Gloria Trefry and Kevin O'Hara
Charles Stewart Mott Senior High School,
Warren, MI, 1977

Sherry Cooper and Mike Lemons
Buffalo High School, Buffalo, MO, 1968

Linda Ponsi and Andrew Kmetz
Copiague High School, Copiague, NY, 1964

George Monte and Virginia Stanley
East Islip High School, East Islip, NY, 1980

Leon Grobaski and Kathy Foley
Cherry Hill High School, Inkster, MI, 1971

Tom McCarthy and Trina Robbins
John Adams High School, Queens, NY, 1955

Jennifer Kalet and Jon Lichtenstein
Scarsdale High School, Scarsdale, NY, 1982

Kristine Kazandjian and Steven Martino
Islip High School, Islip, NY, 1984

Tracy Gerard and Kenny Eisenhardt
Butler High School, Butler, NJ, 1981

Daniel Mailliard and Maureen Koenig
Mercy High School, Omaha, NE, 1984

ABOVE AND OPPOSITE: **Andrew Kmetz and Linda Ponsi**
Copiague High School, Copiague, NY, 1963

Judy Adelfon (center) and friends
Marblehead High School, Marblehead, MA, 1962

Gerry Schorr, Judi Morell, Diane Pettingell, and Don Ransford
Rich Township High School, Park Forest, IL, 1955

Jill Allen and Warren Calvert
Van Horn High School, Independence, MO, 1977

Julie Dito and Steve O'Brien,
Mills High, Millbrae, CA, 1982

Anthony Oliviera, Mikyla Bruder, Jonelle Chase, and Matt Walbeck
Sacramento High School, Sacramento, CA, 1985

Frank Demeri, Tommy Engelhardt, Jeff Weissman,
name unknown, and Robert Defillipo
John F. Kennedy High School, Plainview, NY, 1981

Marshall Reinsdorf, Joan Pachner, Simone Weissman, and Warren Wake
Scarsdale High School, Scarsdale, NY, 1974

The Bongos
George County High School, Lucedale, MI, 1981

Donald Stevenson (back row, 4th from right) and friends
Steel High School, Steelton, PA, 1956

Alvin Stein and Arlene Cohen
(at right) and friends
City College,
New York, NY, 1954

London Central High School,
Hertz, England, 1966

Tina Goldstein (seated 2nd from left) and friends
John F. Kennedy High School, Plainview, NY, 1981

Dean Mellis and Mari Blank
Massapequa High School, Massapequa, NY, 1981

Shari Rotstein and Kevin Ash
Massapequa High School, Massapequa, NY, 1981

OPPOSITE AND ABOVE: **Larry Mehringer and Carla Drago**
Massapequa High School, Massapequa, NY, 1981

Name unknown and Tim Kelly
Sault Collegiate Institute
Sault Ste. Marie, Ontario, Canada, 1973

Fred Fricker and Kathleen Niemer
Milford High School, Milford, OH, 1970

Ruth Victor and
Albert Goldberg (left)
and friends
Brooklyn College,
Brooklyn, NY, 1955

The Last Rou

Kathy Wilson and Jay Harris
Industrial High School, Vanderbilt, TX, 1977

Kathy Wilson and John Douglas
Fairfield High School, Fairfield, TX, 1980

Sue Hodges
Boca Raton High School, Boca Raton, FL, 1968

Lisa Scharak
Mamaroneck High School, Mamaroneck, NY, 1967

Erica Stein
Massapequa High School,
Massapequa, NY, 1987

Dean Mellis
Massapequa High School, Massapequa, NY, 1981

the Prom Whether or not you had the time of your life, it's most likely a night that's forever seared into your memory. And whether or not you really want to relive that high school rite of passage, there will always be evidence of the event in those photos that someone thought to snap—capturing you alone, you with your date, you in your living room, you on your front steps, you and your best friends, you in your first car. Pictures of you and all the girls, you and your proud parents, you and your dog. All the boys. All the couples. Table shots. Formal shots. The one constant being your fabulous outfit. Not to mention your fabulous hair.

When I first started compiling photos for this book, getting people to track down and share their photos seemed to be an impossible quest. But I kept e-mailing and calling and posting, and one by one they trickled in, along with sometimes charming and sometimes appalling stories. Like Rob (pages 34–35), whose first date with Paula was to the prom—they were married for twenty-nine years. Or Lisa (page 91), whose mom made her wear a mod zebra-print mini dress when all she wanted was to look like a sleek Jackie O. Or Kathy (pages 88–89), who sent me not only photos, but invitations, programs, seating cards, and newspaper clippings. And Warren (page 62), who sent his photo, plus photos of all his kids at their proms. I heard about John (page 43), who split his pants while dancing and spent the rest of the night trying desperately to hold the front and back together, and Kathleen (page 85), who used so much hairspray that she got stuck to the inside of a hair dryer and had to be cut out. Not to mention Heather, whose mother said, "Oh honey, you looked so awful at your prom I threw those photos out years ago."

And then there's my prom weekend—it started with a car accident and ended with a Coast Guard rescue.

My gratitude and endless thanks go out to those who shared their photos and stories and made this book what it is—a celebration of memories and fashion statements that made the prom a night to remember.   —*Elissa Stein*

photographers unknown except as follows: